Ancient Egyptian Civilization

Pharaohs and Dynasties
of Ancient Egypt

By Kristine Carlson Asselin

raintree
a Capstone company — publishers for children

Raintree is an imprint of Capstone Global Library Limited, a company incorporated in England and Wales having its registered office at 264 Banbury Road, Oxford, OX2 7DY – Registered company number: 6695582

www.raintree.co.uk
myorders@raintree.co.uk

Edited by Brenda Haugen
Designed by Juliette Peters
Picture research by Svetlana Zhurkin
Production by Laura Manthe

ISBN 978 1 4747 1728 1
19 18 17 16 15
10 9 8 7 6 5 4 3 2 1

British Library Cataloguing in Publication Data
A full catalogue record for this book is available from the British Library.

Photo Credits
Alamy: North Wind Picture Archives, 25; Art Resource, N.Y.: ©The Trustees of the British Museum, 19, Borromeo, 12; The Bridgeman Art Library: ©Look and Learn/Private Collection/Peter Jackson, 4, National Geographic Image Collection/Herbert M. Herget, 9, Photo ©Christie's Images/Private Collection/Reginald Arthur, 22; Capstone: Peter Wilks, 11; Corbis: Gianni Dagli Orti, 18, National Geographic Society, 21; Mary Evans Picture Library, 15, 17; Newscom: akg-images/François Guénet, 6, 10; Shutterstock: artform, cover (hieroglyphs used throughout book), Fedor Selivanov, hieroglyphs used as design element throughout book, GSK, cover (statue), javarman, 16, Kharidehal Abhirama Ashwin, 28, Matej Hudovernik, 29, Mikhail Dudarev, pyramids image used as design element throughout book, Rafa Irusta, papyrus used as design element throughout book, R-studio, cover (gold texture); Superstock Inc: Christie's Images Ltd., 26

We would like to thank Jennifer Houser Wegner, PhD, for her invaluable help in the preparation of this book.

Every effort has been made to contact copyright holders of material reproduced in this book. Any omissions will be rectified in subsequent printings if notice is given to the publisher.

All the internet addresses (URLs) given in this book were valid at the time of going to press. However, due to the dynamic nature of the internet, some addresses may have changed, or sites may have changed or ceased to exist since publication. While the author and publisher regret any inconvenience this may cause readers, no responsibility for any such changes can be accepted by either the author or the publisher.

Printed and bound in China.

CONTENTS

Note to readers:

The years in parentheses after a pharaoh's name are the years the pharaoh ruled Egypt.

Important discovery

Imagine a powerful king who talks with the gods. If the gods are angered, everyone in the country is punished. The fate of the people rests on the king's shoulders alone.

An Egyptian king at a festival.

On the banks of the River Nile in 1897, **archaeologists** discovered a 5,000-year-old **artefact** called the Narmer Palette. Carvings of a powerful king overpowering an enemy decorate the ceremonial plate. At the same time, archaeologists discovered an ancient weapon called a mace. Detailed carvings of royal life appear on the mace head. These artefacts are two of the earliest examples of recorded history. Together, they tell of the beginnings of a civilization. This civilization survived for thousands of years under the leadership of godlike kings called pharaohs.

archaeologist scientist who studies how people lived in the past

artefact object used in the past that was made by people

Call me nesu

The Egyptian word for king was *nesu*. The word *pharaoh* is Greek. The origin of the word pharaoh is *per-aa*, meaning "great house". This term for palace became the term for king in about 1450 BC. The ancient Egyptians did not use the term pharaoh.

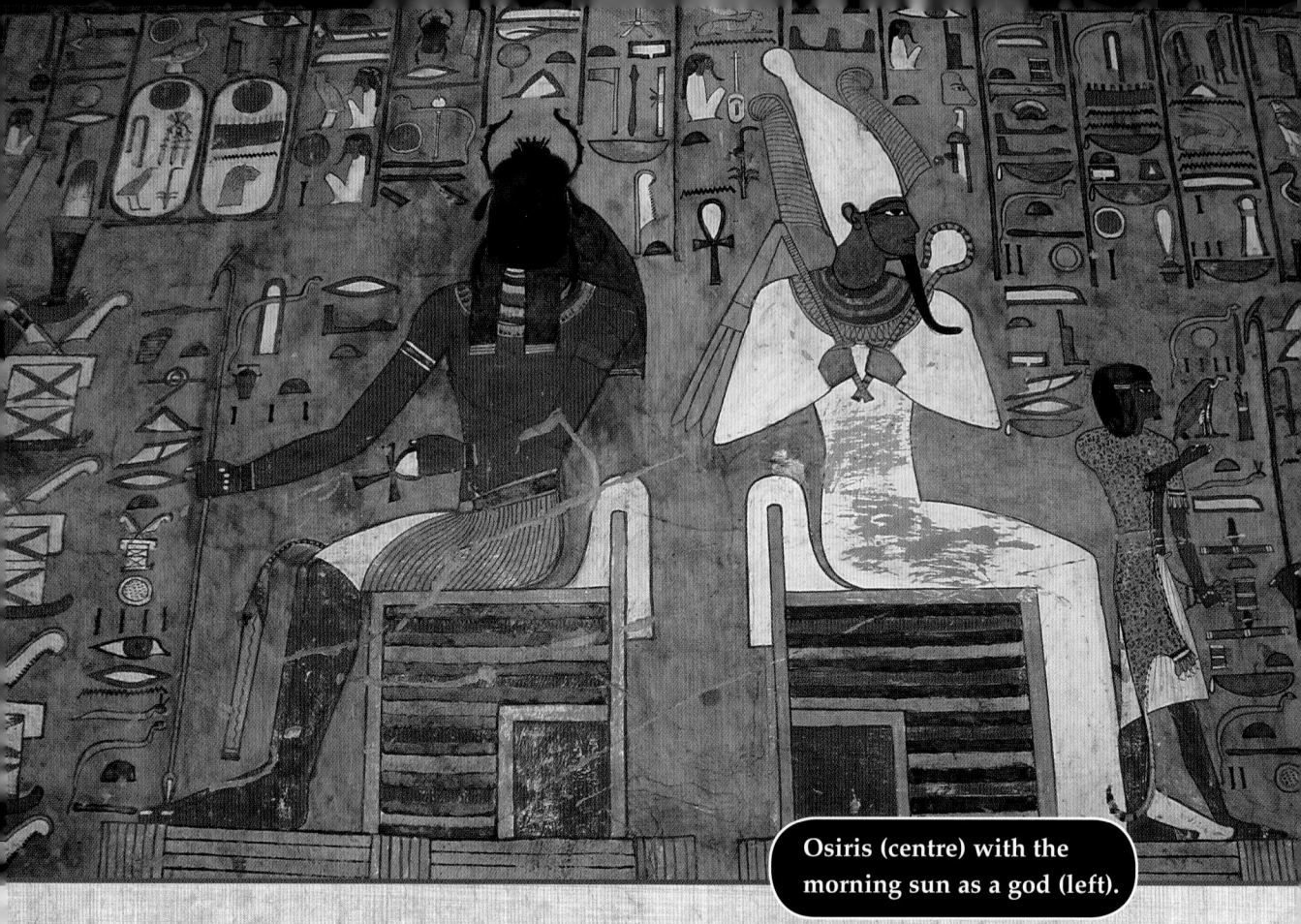

Osiris (centre) with the morning sun as a god (left).

Ancient Egyptians believed King Osiris civilized the land around the River Nile. Myths told of his talent for teaching the people to make bread and wine. He created the first laws. But his brother, Seth, wanted to be king. He killed Osiris to take the throne. Osiris' only son, Horus, avenged his father's death by defeating Seth and taking his rightful place as pharaoh. All pharaohs who ruled Egypt considered themselves descendants of Horus. The ancient Egyptians worshipped their pharaohs as rulers descended from gods.

Pharaohs protected their kingdoms by keeping order. If a pharaoh failed, ancient Egyptians believed the world would fall into chaos. Chaos often meant war with enemy nations. But it could also be a natural disaster or anything that caused widespread misfortune. The fate of the ancient Egyptians' world rested on the pharaoh's shoulders.

The pharaoh was the human link between the gods and people. The gods gave pharaohs their power. The pharaoh communicated with the other gods through offerings, rituals and the building of temples.

The people believed that their pharaoh's efforts brought blessings from the gods. Because of the leadership of more than 170 pharaohs, the ancient Egyptian civilization, which began around 3000 BC, lasted for more than 3,000 years.

chaos total confusion

ritual action that is always done the same way

Chapter 1

Pharaoh:
the destiny of Egypt

Over 5,000 years ago, two kingdoms sprang up along the River Nile and struggled for power. The Egyptian **monarchy** began when these two kingdoms united under one ruler. The first pharaoh is often called Narmer. The Narmer Palette and mace head tell the story of how the first pharaoh came to power.

The pharaoh served as the head of state, the leader in times of war and the chief priest of each god's temple. The pharaoh had complete control over his subjects. But only certain people were born to be pharaoh.

monarchy system of government in which the ruler is a king or queen

Family rule

The title of pharaoh was usually handed down from father to son. But royal wives and daughters played important roles in how a pharaoh came to power. Pharaohs often had several wives. Only one was considered the Great Wife. The Great Wife's children

Queen Nefertiti and King Akhenaten honour a favoured subject.

were the **heirs** to the throne. If she only had daughters, the son of another wife could become pharaoh. But that son had to marry a daughter of the Great Wife, one of his half-sisters. Sometimes, a pharaoh would invite his heir to rule with him as a co-ruler. Pharaohs were usually male, but at least three women ruled Egypt.

heir child who has been, or will be, left a title, property or money

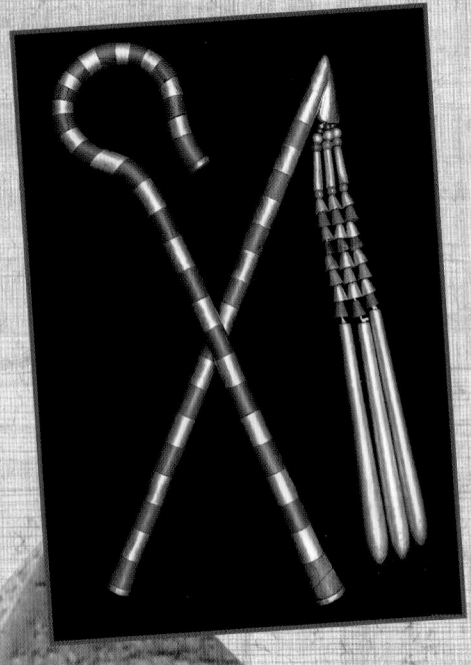

A crook and flail were symbols of royal power.

As a god-king, the pharaoh commanded power and resources over all of Egypt. When a pharaoh wore the ceremonial symbols of the position, the people believed the god Horus was speaking. A pharaoh's symbols included a crook and flail. The crook was symbolic of the pharaoh's role as shepherd of the people. The flail looked like a whip and symbolized supreme power.

The myths of ancient Egyptians were an important part of their history and religion. Egyptians believed their most legendary gods were the first pharaohs. The figures of Ra, the Sun god, and Osiris, the god of the afterlife, were models for all pharaohs to follow. All pharaohs were thought to be the human form of Horus, the falcon god and son of Osiris, and ruled for life.

afterlife life that begins when a person dies

Many crowns

Pharaohs had several crowns, each with a different meaning. A white crown represented Upper Egypt, in the South. A red crown referred to Lower Egypt, around the Nile delta. Worn together, the crowns symbolized a united Egypt.

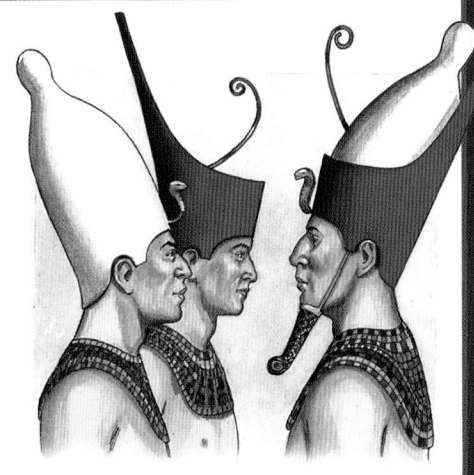

FACT

A cobra ready to strike an enemy was pictured on the front of the king's crown. A king was often shown holding weapons. These weapons were symbols of his role in maintaining order, which included protecting the land from invaders.

King Tutankhamun's tomb.

Upon accepting the throne from the previous pharaoh, the new pharaoh had an important first job. The new pharaoh was responsible for burying the pharaoh he or she replaced. It took three months and a team of workers to prepare the body and put the final touches on the tomb.

The pharaoh's next important duty was to keep away chaos. Chaos in ancient Egypt often took the form of foreign enemies. To protect his people from enemies, a pharaoh made offerings to the gods to keep Egypt in their good favour. Ancient Egyptians believed these offerings not only kept enemies away, but also caused the Nile to flood. An annual flood ensured a bountiful harvest and order for Egypt.

The pharaoh also made important decisions about laws, trade and relationships with foreign countries. If the pharaoh did not succeed in his tasks, the people believed the gods would be angry and punish Egypt.

On more than one occasion, a pharaoh failed to maintain order. When this happened, the government collapsed. It sometimes took many years to rebuild the government. During times of government collapse, a different family – called a dynasty – took control of the throne.

FACT

Today's scholars disagree about the order of some of the pharaohs and family dynasties. Over time, record keeping became disorganized, and some records have been lost.

Chapter 2

The royal families of Egypt

The ancient Egyptians did not use a traditional calendar. But they did mark the seasons. They also counted the years a pharaoh ruled. They marked the passage of time by counting the dynasties. In 3,000 years, 32 dynasties and 170 pharaohs ruled Egypt. Historians group these dynasties into three time periods: Old Kingdom, Middle Kingdom and New Kingdom. Between each kingdom, hundreds of years of unrest gripped the country. Pharaohs ruled during those times, but they were weak leaders who did not unite the people. Only strong leadership could re-establish order.

Narmer

The Old Kingdom

The earliest kings of the Old Kingdom ruled before records of dynasties were kept. Narmer united Upper and Lower Egypt. His story is captured in **hieroglyphs** on the ancient Narmer Palette and mace head. Narmer's reign marks the beginning of a united Egypt.

The Old Kingdom (2625–2130 BC) is considered the golden age of ancient Egypt. During these early dynasties, pharaohs had the Great Pyramids built. Art, building design and writing flourished. Pharaohs had great wealth and power. But the good times did not last. Years of low rainfall caused **famine** across the country. Local governors struggled for power after the death of King Pepi II. The Old Kingdom ended in unrest.

FACT

The Great Pyramid was made of 2.3 million stone blocks. Each block weighed between 2.3 and 13.6 tonnes.

hieroglyph picture or symbol used in the ancient Egyptian system of writing

famine serious shortage of food resulting in widespread hunger and death

Famous pharaohs of the Old Kingdom

The Old Kingdom begins with the Fourth Dynasty. The Pharaoh Khufu (2589–2566 BC) is best known for building the Great Pyramid at Giza. It was the largest pyramid. Until the 19th century, the Great Pyramid was the tallest structure in the world. Khufu's family members were known for being great builders. Khufu's father, Snefru, and Khufu's son, Khafre, also built pyramids.

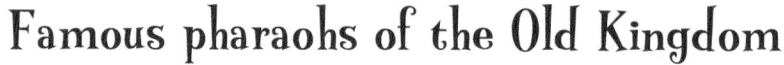

Khafre's pyramid at Giza.

Pepi I, father of Pepi II.

Pepi II (2278–2184 BC) was the longest-reigning king in history. Pepi became pharaoh when he was 6 years old. While Pepi was a child, his mother, Ankhnesmerire II, and uncle, Djau, probably served as regents. Pepi reigned for 94 years, living to be about 100 years old. He was known for starting new relationships with foreign countries. He was the last pharaoh of the Sixth Dynasty and of the Old Kingdom.

regent person who rules a country when the king or queen is too young to do so

The Middle Kingdom

After the disorder at the end of the Old Kingdom calmed, the Middle Kingdom (2040–1782 BC) began. A family of strong leaders took control and re-established order. During these dynasties, written language became more coordinated. Several important texts were written. New technology led to bronze work and pottery. New inventions included looms, used to weave cloth. New musical instruments were also invented.

Mentuhotep II

Famous pharaohs of the Middle Kingdom

The Middle Kingdom saw several famous pharaohs come to power. Mentuhotep II (2061–2010 BC) united Egypt and drove enemy forces out of the country. His family is credited with starting the Middle Kingdom.

Amenemhet I (1985–1955 BC) took the throne from a pharaoh who had no heir. He became the first pharaoh of the 12th Dynasty. He moved the capital of Egypt from Thebes in the south to Itj-tawy in the north.

Queen Sobeknefru (1799–1794 BC) was one of the few female rulers of Egypt. There are few records of her rule. Scholars believe her husband had been pharaoh and that she came to power after he died. As a female pharaoh, she was respected in the same way as a male king.

During the last dynasty of the Middle Kingdom, pharaohs didn't last long. These short reigns weakened the power of the throne. In time, the Middle Kingdom failed because enemy forces overthrew the government and gained power. Invaders took over Lower Egypt and crowned themselves kings.

When the enemies were finally defeated by a dynasty of warrior kings, Egypt reclaimed the throne. The pharaohs of this time built manned forts in northern towns to protect Egypt. The New Kingdom was born.

The New Kingdom

The New Kingdom (1550–1069 BC) spans nearly 500 years of Egyptian history. With their power and wealth, the pharaohs of this time truly were almost godlike people. They left behind art, treasures and themselves – as mummies. During this time, kings' tombs were cut into desert rock cliffs in the Valley of the Kings. The mummies of many kings of the New Kingdom have been found in these tombs.

Famous Pharaohs of the New Kingdom

One of the most famous pharaohs of the New Kingdom was Queen Hatshepsut (1473–1458 BC). She took power after her father, Thutmose I. Hatshepsut dressed like a king and even wore a false beard. During her rule, Egypt flourished with new building projects. She also expanded trade with other nations.

During their reign, Akhenaten and Nefertiti (1352–1336 BC) brought new ideas to Egypt. As king and queen, they rejected the old Egyptian traditions. Akhenaten embraced a new god – Aten – who was shown as a falcon with a sun on its head.

Most people today know the name King Tut. King Tutankhamun, or King Tut, (1336–1327 BC) is famous because of his tomb. The discovery of this tomb in 1922 gave archaeologists a peek inside the pharaoh's world.

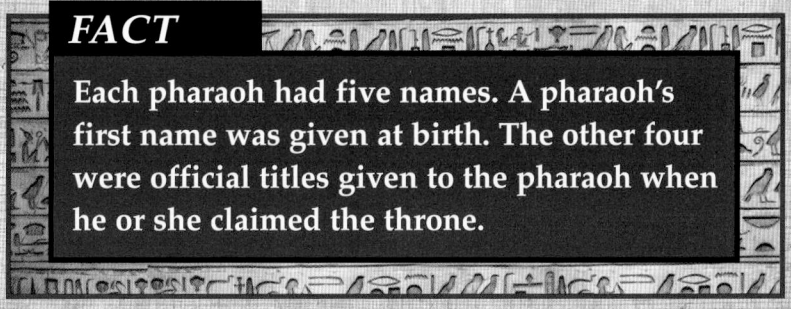

Queen Hatshepsut

Rameses II (1279–1213 BC) was known as Rameses the Great. He lived to be 96 years old and is rumoured to have had 200 wives and more than 100 children. He had two main queens, Nefertari and Istnofret, who were the mothers of his heirs. Rameses was known for his building projects and his wars to keep Syria out of Egypt.

FACT

Each pharaoh had five names. A pharaoh's first name was given at birth. The other four were official titles given to the pharaoh when he or she claimed the throne.

Viziers were often with a pharaoh to help him when needed.

Pharaohs lived very different lives to the common people. Servants woke the pharaohs in the morning. They bathed and dressed the pharaohs before breakfast. Black paint called kohl was painted on the pharaohs' eyelids, and gold pendants hung round their necks. Pharaohs were often carried in a chair by servants.

Egypt's pharaohs had absolute authority over everyone and everything. But they also had help. Educated assistants carried out the pharaoh's wishes. They also helped run the palace's day-to-day activities. The king's main assistants were called viziers. They helped make decisions.

vizier important government official

The pharaoh was the high priest in every temple across the country and led important rituals. But the pharaoh could not be in every temple all the time. Other priests handled the daily activities in the temples on the pharaoh's behalf. They helped organize festivals and led religious rituals.

Ancient Egyptians spent most of their lives preparing for the afterlife. The pharaoh prepared for his own death by creating a resting place for his body. Not all kings built pyramids. In fact, the largest and most famous pyramids were all built during the Fourth Dynasty. Later pharaohs preferred hidden tombs.

After death, a pharaoh's body was prepared for the afterlife. The body was **mummified** and buried with everyday objects needed for a happy life. These objects often included weapons, jewellery, furniture and games. Some pharaohs were even buried with their horses and chariots.

mummify preserving a body with special salts and cloth to make it last for a very long time

Chapter 3

The end of the pharaohs

The ancient Egyptian civilization lasted longer than any other in history. Its art and culture affected other societies which developed in the ancient world. Eventually, foreign powers invaded the Nile valley.

The rulers of the 22nd, 23rd and 24th Dynasties came from Libya, though their families had lived in Egypt for generations. Nubian kings conquered Egypt and ruled during the 25th Dynasty. In 332 BC, Alexander the Great of Macedonia marched into Egypt. He defeated the Persians, who had conquered Egypt in the 27th Dynasty. The Egyptian people considered Alexander the Great their rescuer.

As the new ruler of Egypt, Alexander made a **pilgrimage** to the temple of Amon. Because it rained during his trip, he believed the gods of Egypt blessed him. Alexander founded the city of Alexandria. It quickly became the centre of art, culture and business in Egypt. Most of the money made in Alexandria at the time was through the export of Egyptian goods.

pilgrimage journey to a holy place for religious reasons

After Alexander died, a series of kings called Ptolemy ruled for the next 300 years. These kings started with Ptolemy I (305–285 BC) and ended with Ptolemy XV. They worked hard to keep Egypt powerful. During their rules, new building projects were completed, including amazing temples and the great library at Alexandria. When the Roman Empire started to gain power, the conquerors set their eyes on wealthy Egypt.

FACT

Nectanebo II, who died in 343 BC, was the last pharaoh born in Egypt.

Old Alexandria

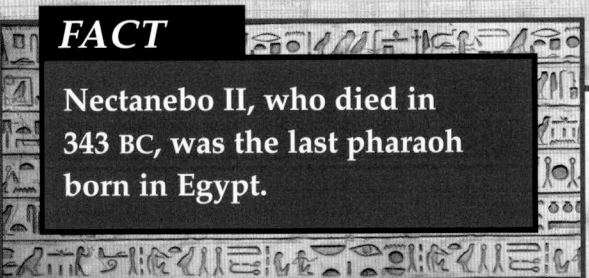

Cleopatra VII

Cleopatra VII (51–30 BC), Egypt's last true pharaoh, came to power as a teenager. Rome was conquering most of the Mediterranean at this time. In an effort to unite Egypt with a powerful ally, Cleopatra became close to the Roman general, Julius Caesar. Under Cleopatra's reign Egypt prospered.

When Caesar was killed, Cleopatra had a relationship with another ally, Mark Antony. He was popular amongst his Roman soldiers and the people of Egypt. But senior Roman leaders lost faith in Mark Antony. He lost several important battles, which made them doubt his loyalty to Rome. With Cleopatra, Mark Antony had wanted to rule over half the known world. In the end, both Cleopatra and Mark Antony died while in power.

After Cleopatra's death, Egypt became a Roman colony. The title of pharaoh was still used. Roman emperors dressed as pharaohs and carried out the ancient rituals.

Even in ancient times, many of the temples and monuments were world famous. But after Christianity became common, temples were closed or converted to churches. Many statues of gods and other artefacts were destroyed. The ancient Egyptian culture faded. Over thousands of years, desert sands buried ancient Egypt.

Pharaohs with direct links to the gods do not rule Egypt anymore. But archaeological discoveries have uncovered their way of life. Historians have been able to piece together the order of the pharaohs, based on ancient texts and lists found in tombs. But there are still many gaps, and experts sometimes disagree. It has not stopped modern storytellers from drawing on the legacy of ancient Egypt for books, films and video games. The pharaohs of ancient Egypt continue to influence the world.

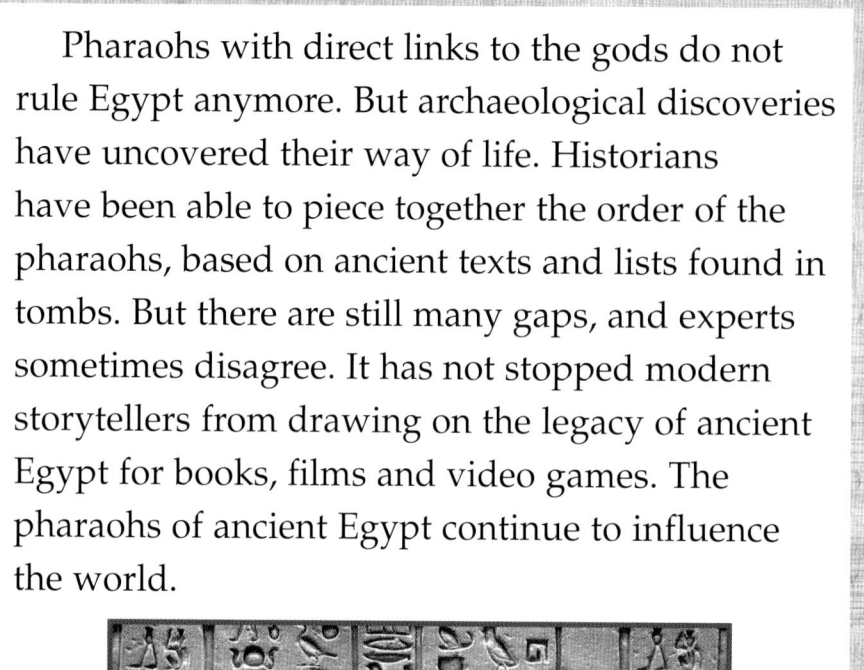

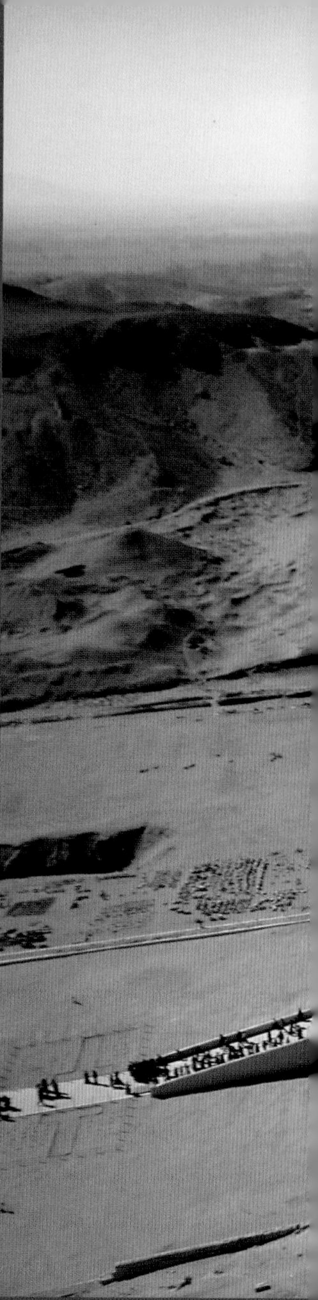

Valley of the Kings and the temple of Queen Hatshepsut.

FACT

The order of the pharaohs' reigns comes from lists found in tombs. Information also comes from the writing of an Egyptian priest named Manetho. He lived during the reign of Ptolemy II. Because some of the lists exclude whole dynasties, historians are unsure if every pharaoh is now known.

GLOSSARY

afterlife life that begins when a person dies

archaeologist scientist who studies how people lived in the past

artefact object used in the past that was made by people

chaos total confusion

famine serious shortage of food resulting in widespread hunger and death

heir child who has been, or will be, left a title, property or money

hieroglyph picture or symbol used in the ancient Egyptian system of writing

monarchy system of government in which the ruler is a king or queen

mummify preserving a body with special salts and cloth to make it last for a very long time

pilgrimage journey to a holy place for religious reasons

regent person who rules a country when the king or queen is too young to do so

ritual action that is always done the same way

vizier important government official

READ MORE

Cleopatra: Powerful Leader or Ruthless Pharaoh? (Perspectives on History), Peggy Caravantes (Raintree, 2015)

Ramesses II (Hero Journals), Richard Spilsbury (Raintree, 2014)

Tomb Explorers (Treasure Hunters), Nicola Barber (Raintree, 2013)

WEBSITES

www.ancientegypt.co.uk/pharaoh/home.html
Learn all about the different pharaohs of ancient Egypt.

www.bbc.co.uk/history/ancient/egyptians
Discover cool facts about pyramids, mummification, gods and goddesses.

INDEX

4/16.